Inclusive Language:

A Writing Guide on Respecting Diversity

Lingo Valley Inc.

TABLE OF CONTENTS

1

INTRODUCTION

Every word has a history and comes from the past. The historical context has an acute bearing on the creation and adaptation of language, and words will innately point to something beyond their principal meaning. The word 'landlord', for example, dates back to Middle English (spoken after the Norman conquest in 1066 until the late 15th Century) and is a combination of land + lord—reflecting common land ownership norms during that time.

Today, land ownership is no longer restricted to the elite echelon of society or male aristocrats. The world has changed. We live in an age when it's more important than ever to think rigorously and sensibly about the words we use and the influence they possess.

Many companies are taking a leading role in breaking with traditional norms and neglect by promoting diversity to create an inclusive work environment. Building an inclusive social and work environment starts with communication, and as the most basic unit of verbal exchange, words are an essential starting point. From online registration forms to blog posts and internal emailing, it's vital that everyone in the organization respects the natural diversity of their audience. This extends but is not limited to race and ethnicity, gender, sexual orientation, people with disabilities, and age.

Failure to respect diversity, including unintended discrimination or insensitive communication, can not only be offensive to other people but can also provoke negative reactions and consequences to reputation (at a personal and organizational level). In addition, digital forms of communication are enhancing awareness of inclusive language while also magnifying the consequences of discrimination, which is extremely difficult to retract.

To avoid mistakes, it's important to self-examine content according to the themes covered in this book. A practical six-point checklist can also be found in Chapter 11.

What is Inclusive Language?

Inclusive language refers to neutral and unbiased language, free from words and phrases that reflect prejudice, stereotyping, or discriminatory views of groups of people. Inclusive language has the goal of embracing people of diverse backgrounds and making them feel a part of the group. Inclusive language is also the opposite of deliberate or unintentional exclusion of people based on aspects regarding their identity.

While there are areas of overlap in the discussion of topics, inclusive language should be distinguished from 'political correctness'. Inclusive language is tied to the value of 'inclusion', giving people a true sense of belonging as well as giving them full access to opportunities, and not excluding anyone. Political correctness, meanwhile, is using language that minimizes disputes or conflict but often conceals the true values of the writer or organization, such as opinions about global warming or territorial disputes.

Political correctness also extends to a diverse range of political topics including the environment, human rights, historical problems, social justice, income equality, and territorial disputes, whereas inclusive language is focused on people and their identity.

In sum, inclusive language comes from a place of genuine acceptance and respect for people, and a conscious effort to communicate in that way, whereas political correctness is less tied to inclusiveness and may even contradict inclusive values. A government or organization's public stance on recognizing Taiwan as a province or territory of the People's Republic of China is viewed as politically correct in many public forums but this stance isn't inclusive to people in Taiwan who identify themselves as citizens of an independent nation state, for example.

Why Inclusive Language is Important

A person's gender, sexual orientation, age, and race are important characteristics of who they are but, of course, don't define who they are. Attempting to reduce a person to a single characteristic of their identity has the potential to cause offense. Adopting inclusive language helps to respect people's unique identities without contributing to existing stereotypes and labels.

The words we use, though, can sometimes be loaded and single out minorities whether we (as the writer or presenter) realize it or not. Thus, the best way to avoid (unintentionally) excluding people, is to consider and choose words carefully, create a reference base of preferred terms, and to follow best practices.

Inclusive language also goes beyond avoiding offense to readers or viewers. Inclusive language is about making content welcoming to a wider audience. If a global company is communicating with a global audience, they don't want to be caught in the habit of communicating in a strong Australian or American tone of voice that uses colloquial terms, local case studies, and only references cities exclusive to the country of their head office. Instead, it's important to present the company as possessing a global mindset that takes into account the needs of a global customer base and demonstrate that through using inclusive language.

Who is this Guide for?

This concise and practical guide to inclusive language applies to anyone who wants to respect diversity through the way they write and speak in the English language. This includes professional content writers or podcasters, business leaders, people working in human resources, community workers, doctors, and virtually every profession where communication plays an important role.

It's vital to treat this book as a summary of recommended practices rather than as a prescriptive instruction manual. There is no universal or fixed rule book when it comes to inclusive language, and any attempt would be futile as language is fluid and ever-changing. Instead, this book provides a roundup of preferred terms and solutions for mitigating non-inclusive language problems such as the use of the male pronoun and unintended or deliberate stereotyping of groups through language.

Your own inclusive language guide and practices should also take into account local considerations such as indigenous groups and national or local history. The term 'invasion', for example, evokes loaded and negative connotations for Aboriginal and Torres Strait Islander peoples in Australia (as the starting point of social exclusion, loss of culture, and the negative impact on their identity), while the same word doesn't convey the same connotation when describing wars fought on the western border of France in the 20th Century or the northern borders of China during the later Middle Ages.

Notes and Key Points on Using this Guide

Language is fluid

As with all types of language, 'inclusive language' is constantly evolving as people find new words that best describe who they are as well as their outward identity. Nowadays, the term 'lifestyle choice' is considered outdated for referring to sexual orientation as it denotes sexual identity as a 'choice'.

Another example is the terms 'master' and 'slave', which have been highlighted in the past as non-inclusive. Corporate organizations didn't begin to replace these terms with inclusive variants until mid-2020 following the murder of George Floyd by police. Due to the cost of replacing terms, it sometimes takes a major public event to jolt organizations into action.

It's therefore important to acknowledge the fluid and changing quality of language and to keep yourself up-to-date with the recent trends or events and adapt to new language and best practices over time.

As a result, the contents of this book are subject to change, and we welcome you to contact us (lingovalley@gmail.com) with suggestions or variations that you consider important to add to this guide and help fellow readers.

The second point to make here is that not everyone will agree. There is no absolute agreement on inclusive language and you will need to consider the following guidelines while also taking into account your own audience, industry, and organization.

Visual content

Providing an inclusive user experience includes images, promotional banners, signs, flyers, and visual-based social media posts. Avoiding cultural stereotyping in visual materials, promoting diversity (in images of people for example), and following inclusive language principles for accompanying text should not be overlooked as part of an inclusive user experience.

Accessibility

Concerning the visual presentation and accessibility of content, it's always important to consider the readability of the text. You want to ensure the size of the text is appropriate and there's sufficient contrast between the text and background color to allow people with low vision to clearly read your content.

Another often overlooked consideration is that approximately 1 in 12 men (8%) and 1 in 200 (0.5%) women are classed as colorblind.[1] Tools like Hue and ColorBrewer (http://colorbrewer2.org/) provide a filter that lets you select from palettes pre-tested for color blindness.

Sources

The research for this book was based exclusively on English-language resources, primarily from Australia, Canada, the United Kingdom, and the United States. Sources included government websites, the World Health Organization, university guides, and peer-reviewed academic papers from the SSRN electronic library.

---

[1] "Colour Blindness," *colourblindnessawareness.org*, viewed January 20, 2019, http://www.colourblindawareness.org/colour-blindness/.

2

THE HACKER'S GUIDE TO INCLUSIVE LANGUAGE

While this guide could hardly be condemned of lengthiness, here we provide a succinct overview of the core ideas and recommendations covered in this book.

1) Avoid assuming a user's race, religion, gender, age, marital status, or sexual orientation.

2) Avoid non-inclusive terms that are male-dominant (i.e. manpower and landlord), racially offensive (i.e. blacklist and slave/master), or disrespectful of older persons (i.e. geriatric and old people) and people with a disability (i.e. crazy and handicapped).

3) Avoid using and subscribing to stereotypes based on age, race, gender, sexual orientation, etc, such as "you complain like an old woman".

4) Choose terms that are widely accepted as inclusive at the time of publication and update your content and inclusive language guide where possible to reflect recent trends.

5) Try to include the greatest number of people possible whenever you communicate.

3

RACIAL EQUALITY & NEUTRALITY

Beyond striving for inclusive language in the domain of race and ethnicity, it's important to consider the unintended meaning of words, including whether they possess racial connotations, and to also familiarize yourself with these words.

As of 2020, major U.S. companies including Twitter and JPMorgan have announced dropping common programming terms in favor of more inclusive language. These terms include 'master', 'slave', 'whitelist', and 'blacklist'. While not intended to refer to the literal meaning of the term in programming speak, the evolution of these words stirs associations to suppression and enslavement.

In computer programming, 'master' refers to a device or process that controls other devices or processes called 'slaves'. 'Blacklist', meanwhile, is used to describe people or items automatically denied from a service, such as forbidden websites or user accounts. Alternative terms include 'allow list' and 'deny list' for 'whitelist' and 'blacklist', and 'primary' and 'replica' for 'master' and 'slave' respectively.

Negative stereotypes can also be created when relying on broad descriptions. If it's necessary to speak about a person's cultural or ethnic background, try to be as specific as possible. Referring to someone as 'Asian' or 'African', for example, overlooks the diverse and unique languages, identities, and cultures throughout those regions. Instead, be detailed and descriptive.

✎ Example

"Sickle cell disease is most common in those of sub-Saharan ancestry", rather than "Sickle cell disease mostly occurs in blacks".

Similarly, people from Asia can be described as citizens of countries in the Far East, Southeast Asia, or the Indian subcontinent.

Where possible, ask the person how they wish to be described based on where they or their family members were born rather than making assumptions.

Likewise, be descriptive and accurate rather than reductive when describing a person's citizenship and immigration status, such as their nationality, country of origin, category of citizenship (permanent resident/temporary resident/citizen), and whether they are undocumented/unauthorized. Additionally, avoid using racially charged or discriminatory language such as 'illegal' and 'alien' to describe people who originate from another country.

The use of 'illegal' can be applied to actions or concepts such as 'illegal immigration' but should not be used to refer to people, e.g. 'illegal immigrant'.

Avoiding Indirect Stereotypes of Race and Ethnicity

Beyond specific words, it's important to avoid projecting negative stereotypes of a given race or country through content narratives and messaging. Take Dolce & Gabanna (D&G) for example, who in 2019 launched a campaign featuring D&G models mingling with poor people in underdeveloped parts of China. The campaign prompted consumers in China to protest the brand was deliberately presenting their country as a third-world nation, and there have been other similar instances in the fashion world that have been seen as supporting negative stereotypes of Asia.

These campaigns not only have the potential to alienate and disappoint viewers but can also negatively affect the brand in those markets. Dolce & Gabbana reported global revenue of $1.5 billion in the year to March 2017, with approximately 30% of that revenue coming from China based on industry norms.

D&G was boycotted in China with e-commerce platforms including xiaohongshu.com, JD.COM, and Alibaba's Tmall temporarily concealing D&G products from their sites. Xiaohongshu.com told the Global Times that "interests of the motherland should not be infringed" and that "all forms of cooperation are based on respect".

The boycott also included hashtags such as "D&G, get out of China" and "D&G insulting China" which went on to gain more than 2 billion views on Chinese social media.

A leaflet held by Chinese people protesting in front of D&G's flagship store in Milan, Italy

Quick Tips:

- Avoid using terms that reinforce racial, ethnic, or religious stereotypes such as 'slave' and 'master'.
- Avoid terms that treat black and white as a negative-positive category, such as 'whitelist' and 'blacklist'.[2]
- Don't assume that an entire race or ethnicity celebrates a specific religious event (i.e. Christmas) or engages in a fixed ethnic behavior.
- Making references to a person's cultural background, ethnicity, and/or faith is generally not necessary.
- When relevant to speak about a person's cultural or ethnic background, try to be specific, and if possible, ask the person how they wish to be described.
- Avoid hyphenating nationalities, e.g. 'Asian Americans', not 'Asian-Americans'. (The use of the hyphen goes back to the late 19th Century and early 20th Century as a way of ridiculing Americans of foreign birth or origin.)
- Do not use geographic descriptions interchangeably with religious or other descriptions. For example, not all Muslims are Arab, and Brazilians who speak Portuguese are Latino but not Hispanic.
- Capitalize the proper noun names of nationalities, peoples, races, and tribes, e.g. Aboriginal Peoples, Métis, Cree, Inuit, Arab, French Canadian, Christian, Jewish, Latin, Asian.
- It's sometimes recommended to avoid terms that associate the color black with a negative meaning such as 'black sheep', 'black magic', 'blackmail', and 'black market'.

---

[2] Note, that at the time of writing, the terms 'white-hat' and 'black-hat' (for describing aboveboard and underhand tactics respectively) haven't gained the same threshold of support as 'whitelist' and 'blacklist' for finding alternative terms. The information security (infosec) community is currently divided on the suspected racial context behind these two terms. There is also an entire conference called the Black Hat Briefings for computer security to take into consideration for a potential renaming.

- The terms 'B(/b)lack' and 'African American' are not always interchangeable as some people do not identify as African and/or American.
- Refer to groups with specific descriptions, such as 'Asian musicians', 'Asian faculty members', 'Asian students', rather than as 'Asians', 'Africans', 'Latinos', etc.
- Consider the need to mention race. Ask yourself: "Would I mention 'white student' or 'white faculty member' in the same situation?

List of preferred terms:

Sample Term	Preferred Equivalent	Sample Term	Preferred Equivalent
whitelist	allowed list | allow list	master	primary
blacklist	blocked list | deny list	slave	replica
Hispanic	Latino	browns	name the group/ethnicity being referenced

15

4

GENDER-INCLUSIVE LANGUAGE

Although gender biased language can be directed in favor of women and against men, historically, it has been directed against women and in favor of men. Gender-inclusive language, which avoids bias, is called 'gender-neutral language', 'non-sexist language', or 'gender-inclusive language'. The opposite, 'gender-biased language, also called 'sexist language', refers to terms and expressions that present men as the standard norm and demeans or trivializes women.

Gender is an important topic today and there are a number of basic guidelines we can follow to promote equality between the sexes.

To start with, keep content gender-neutral (where possible) and avoid stereotypes based on genders, such as women in the role of the housewife and office receptionist.

Next, when discussing professions, try to remove gender terms from the job title such as fireman, policeman, and businessman. Instead, use firefighter, police officer, and business executive, which are gender-inclusive variants and inclusive of female professionals.

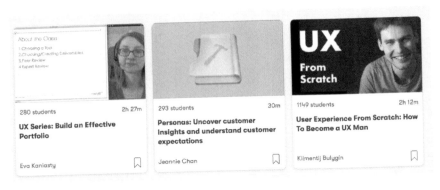

Source: Skillshare.com

In the screenshot above, we can see a course available on the online learning platform, Skillshare.com, titled **"User Experience From Scratch: How to Become a UX Man"**. While the contents of this online course applies to people of both genders, the title may discourage females to click on the thumbnail—especially as the image is also of a man. The thumbnail image does not need to contain a woman or even both genders, but in this case, it might inflate the user's suspicion that the course is designed for males or male-centric in content. It's worth noting that the course creator is not a native English speaker, his business is called UXMAN Design Studio, and the picture is of him.

As another quick side note, the words to describe a job position can also impact the likelihood of that position appealing to men or women. Studies have found that the terms 'independent', 'dominant', and 'fast-paced' are terms that commonly appeal to male applicants but which, quantitively speaking, repel women from applying. Instead, women are more likely to respond to positions that speak of 'collaboration', 'supportive', and 'cooperation' in their descriptions. While none of these words are discriminating in meaning, it's important to consider this phenomenon and aim for language that is balanced and appeals equally to men and women.

Pronouns

Pronouns such as 'he', 'him', and 'his' are common examples of positioning the masculine as the general norm for referring to a person of unspecified sex, such as: "a football player should lead his team from the front". This use of the masculine pronoun 'his' is gender-biased in this example because professional and amateur female players can be both men and women and underlines how pronouns treat males as the norm by omitting references to females.

Omitting reference to women from a generic noun such as 'football player', 'lawyer' or 'priest' through the use of pronouns has the effect of excluding the feminine from the discourse (by way of the audience's imagination or consciousness).

The use of the masculine gender to refer to people of unspecified sex is, in fact, a relatively recent development. Concerned about the increasing acceptance of 'they' as a singular pronoun, grammar specialists in the 18th Century proposed generic masculine pronouns including 'he' as a singular pronoun for referring to a 'man' or 'woman'. The grammar specialists in question are reported to have been male and reasoned on the lines that reflected their male-dominant world; the masculine includes or embraces the feminine.

This gender-bias built on the earlier work of William Lily. As the author of a widely used Latin grammar textbook in England and the first high master of St Paul's School in London, Lily wrote in 1567, "Where note, That the Masculine Gender is more worthy than the Feminine, and the Feminine more worthy than the Neuter".

While the Bible was rewritten in gender-neutral language in the late 19th Century by Julia Smith and Elizabeth Stanton, this trend continued largely unbroken until the late 20th Century. As recent as 1975, nearly all American junior and senior high school grammar books mandated generic masculine pronouns.

Solutions

A common solution to the gender pronoun problem is to use the plural forms 'their', 'they', and 'them', which tends to be more common in informal speech.

✎ Example

"When you find the responsible person, tell **them** to pay me a visit".

While this solution helps to avoid gender bias, it can be confusing as to whether the plural pronoun refers to a generic person or a group. In the used example, the inclusion of "person" indicates the speaker is referring to a generic person. However, if we change "person" to "party" the intent is difficult to discern, as "party" can refer to an individual or a group of people.

✎ Example

"When you find the responsible **party**, tell them to pay me a visit".

Moreover, this solution is less appropriate for formal writing in an academic, legal, or business context. Another solution is to take a singular noun and use the plural version, which invites the use of a plural pronoun.

✎ Example

"A developer should keep his code clean and standard" becomes "Developers should keep **their** code clean and standard".

Alternatively, we could update the sample sentence to remove the use of a pronoun using passive tense.

✎ Example

"In the developer world, it's best practice to keep code clean and standard".

Passive sentences, though, are generally wordier, vaguer, and avoided by some writers and style guides.
The next solution is to alternate the pronouns to avoid the generic masculine.

✎ Example

"When a writer puts his audience first, the reader is more likely to recommend his work to her friends".

Again, though, this workaround can be confusing and unnecessary and adds the hazard of inadvertently reinforcing gender stereotypes, i.e. writers are men, and readers are female, or it's usually females and not males who recommend books to friends.

Treicher and Frank, however, recommend this approach "if done carefully" where there is no danger of reinforcing gender stereotypes. Some authors, including Seth Godin, also do away with the male pronoun for generic situations and consistently use the female pronoun. As a reverse tactic to using the male pronoun, this method—more than any other—serves to highlight feminine issues but, technically speaking, is not a long-term solution for setting a culture of inclusive language.

In place of alternating pronouns, a widely preferred solution is to pair gender-based pronouns.

✎ Example

"When a writer puts his or her audience first mind, the reader is more likely to recommend the book to others".

This approach ticks the box for the inclusion of both genders but can slow down the momentum or flow of the writing and especially for sentences with multiple pronouns.

✎ Example

"When a writer puts his or her audience first mind, the reader is more likely to recommend the book to his or her friends".

The use of paired gender-based pronouns draws the reader's attention to the intent of the writer in using gender-inclusive language which may distract them from the core intent of the writing. A product description page, for example, should focus on converting the user to click "buy" rather than highlighting the issue of gender-bias in modern language.

In other situations, though, it might be more appropriate to use paired pronouns. A university brochure for prospective students, for instance, can promote an inclusive study environment using paired gender-based pronouns in their copy.

Another option to bypass the use of pronouns is to repeat the noun.

✎ Example

"If a writer does meet his deadline, the writer won't get paid".

This style of writing is less acceptable for formal writing and can come across as sneering or negative.

The final option discussed in this chapter is the creation of alternative gender pronouns such as 'ze' and 'zir' as alternatives for 'he/her' and 'he/him', and 'zie/hir' for 'they/them'. These alternative options, while used in some circles, haven't reached a critical threshold to be accepted by many inclusive language guides at a university or government level. In fact, there have been many suggested alternatives for gender pronouns as listed on Wikipedia (https://en.wikipedia.org/wiki/Third-person_pronoun#Alternation_of_she_and_he).

In summary, all of the methods mentioned help to avoid gender bias, and, when used correctly, are usually invisible to the reader. However, as noted, there are minor drawbacks to each of these techniques, and repeatedly relying on some methods can be distracting and introduce confusion in the mind of the reader. Writers, therefore, need to strike a balance between omitting pronouns altogether or explicitly drawing the reader's attention to gender-based language by using paired gender-based pronouns or feminine pronouns, for example.

Gender-marked Roles

Another form of gender-bias language in English arises with gender-marked roles such as 'waitress', 'chairman', and 'fireman' which omit reference to the feminine even though these roles can be performed by persons of both genders. While such roles may have traditionally been exclusive to a given gender, gender-marked roles are mostly redundant today and have the effect of trivializing or ignoring the reality of both sexes performing the role. These terms can be simply substituted with neutral replacements such as 'waiter', 'chairperson', and 'firefighter'.

Gender Titles

The gender titles of 'Miss' and 'Mrs.' present a unique problem. While neither term is discriminatory in their literal meaning, the absence of a male equivalent produces unfair judgment. While the female titles of 'Miss' and 'Mrs.' effectively recognize a woman's marital status, there is no such equivalent title for men, as Mr. applies to both married and unmarried men.

As a counter solution to this discrepancy, 'Ms.' —as the closest equivalent to 'Mr'—is commonly used to reference both unmarried and married women (so as not to identify the subject's marital status).

Formality

The next type of gender-biased language is found in references to females in a demeaning or trivializing way such as a 'girl' or 'sweetie' in reference to an adult woman. Linguist Deborah Cameron explains that when used by people who aren't closely acquainted with the subject, these terms "are inherently disrespectful. They are a unilateral declaration by the man that he need not trouble about the formalities expected between non-intimates".[3]

Objections

---

[3]

The following are common objectives put forward against gender-neutral language and advocacy.

1) **Tradition:** well-established language patterns should not be changed as breaking with tradition induces confusion and problems at both an individual and societal level.

2) **Triviality:** the issue of gender-based language is trivial when considering the effort of updating norms and existing content to reflect what is currently accepted—thereby outweighing the associated benefits.

3) **Aesthetics:** gender-neutral language is generally less concise and may be unnecessarily complicated, e.g. 'weatherman' versus 'weather forecaster'. Gender-neutral language may also affect the flow of the sentence especially as female and male pronouns are used for each example, i.e. "he or she should not put his or her life down for a trivial cause".[4]

4) **Contentious:** gender-neutral language may aggravate people who do not support the values, motivation, and grounds of inclusiveness in language. Canadian university professor, Jordan Peterson, for example, has argued against gender-neutral pronouns, including 'ze' and 'zir' as alternatives to 'he' and 'she', as limiting freedom of speech and as a pretext for political propaganda.

Quick Tips:

- In examples where you refer to two people as an example, use both a female name (Stephanie) and a male name (Steve).
- Avoid 'guys' to refer to mixed-gender groups.

Deborah Cameron, 'Feminism and Linguistic Theory', *Palgrave Macmillan*, 2nd Edition, 1992.

- For gender-neutral scenarios, use 'they' and 'their' as singular or collective pronouns.
- Avoid the use of pronouns for generic situations if appropriate.

Traditional Masculine	He sent a gift card	I messaged him	I received his message
Traditional Feminine	She sent a gift card	I messaged her	I received her message
Gender Neutral	They sent a gift card	I messaged them	I received their message

- Avoid guessing marital status. When in doubt, reconsider the need to include this information.
- Avoid male-centric words such as manpower, man-hours, one-man show, salesman, etc. See an extended list below.

List of preferred terms:

Sample Term	Preferred Equivalent	Sample Term	Preferred Equivalent
manpower	workforce | staffing	policeman	police person
man-hours	work hours	girlfriend | boyfriend	partner
salesman	salesperson	husband | wife	spouse
landlord	owner	mankind	humankind
maiden name	family name	congressman	legislator
husband | wife	spouse or partner	mother | father	parent
different sex	opposite sex	guys	folks
mankind	humankind	weather man	weather forecaster
Miss | Mrs.	Ms.	waitress	waiter
manmade	artificial | synthetic | constructed	forefathers	ancestors
manning the office	staffing the office	chairman	chair (person)
ombudsman	ombuds	freshman	first-year

or long documents, books, websites, and other large compilations of
xt, it's sometimes useful to search within Microsoft Word, the web
owser, or another interface for the word "man" using the search tool.
his will help to quickly find words such as 'manpower', 'mankind',
nan-hours', and so on.

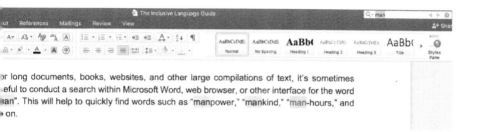

or long documents, books, websites, and other large compilations of text, it's sometimes
eful to conduct a search within Microsoft Word, web browser, or other interface for the word
nan". This will help to quickly find words such as "manpower," "mankind," "man-hours," and
 on.

xample of searching for terms in Microsoft Word

5

SEXUAL ORIENTATION & IDENTITY

Similar to gender-inclusive language, sexual orientation language benefits from avoiding stereotypes and assumptions. As an example, we shouldn't assume that a person assigned a gender at birth identifies with that gender, and we should therefore be careful not to misreport their identified gender.

The next important consideration is word choice. Perhaps more than any other section in this book, sexual orientation and identity are subject to change as formally accepted words and phrases become outdated and offensive in the future or even vice versa in some cases.

At the time of writing, words such as 'prejudice' or 'bias' are preferred over the use of 'homophobia,' 'equal rights' or 'civil rights for gay people' over 'gay rights', and 'assigned/designated male/female at birth' over 'born a man/woman'.

In general, try to use broad terms to discuss relationship status such as 'partner' or 'spouse' in place of 'boyfriend', 'girlfriend', etc. Partner and spouse are broader terms as they can be applied to different forms of relationships and are less assumptive of the subject. In each case, you also need to consider whether it's even necessary to mention marital or relationship status.

When people are legally recognized as married, 'husband' or 'wife' can be used unless specified by the couple.

Explanation of Commonly Accepted Terms

LGBTQ: The popular term LGBTQ offers a useful guide for referring to people who are lesbian, gay, bisexual, transgender, and queer or questioning.

The term LGBTQ can also be used to refer to people who identify with this community. This term should be used over the 'gay community' unless strictly referring to a community of gay men. Keep in mind, too, that you cannot refer to someone as an 'LGBTQ person' as this term is an umbrella term rather than a specific description of an individual person.

Straight: This is a widely accepted term to describe someone who is 'heterosexual' (which is another widely accepted term).

Bisexual: A person who is attracted to people of more than one gender. In general, avoid the term 'bi' as this term is not as well accepted as 'bisexual' at a formal level.

Lesbian: A woman who is attracted to other women.

Gay: People attracted to those of the same sex. To delineate between men and women, use 'gay men' and 'lesbians'. Do not use 'gay' as a singular noun, such as "He is gay". Instead, use "He is a gay man". It's acceptable, though, to use 'gays' as a plural noun, such as "Gays celebrate landmark court case".

Lastly, avoid the term 'homosexual' in all forms, i.e. 'homosexual relationship', 'homosexual man', 'homosexual couple', etc.

Queer: This is a term for those who are not heterosexual/straight or cisgender (a term for people whose gender identity matches their sex assigned at birth). Some people use 'queer' to describe their gender and sexual orientation when other terms do not fit.

While used as a discriminatory term against those with same-sex desires or relationships in the late 19th Century, the term has become accepted over the last 40 years by queer activists including Queer Nation, who tend to be more politically radical than other branches of the LGBT community.

For context, the Queer Nation, formed in the year 1990, circulated an anonymous flier at the New York Gay Pride Parade titled "Queers Read This" providing the following explanation of the term 'queer':

"Ah, do we really have to use that word? It's trouble. Every gay person has his or her own take on it. For some, it means strange and eccentric and kind of mysterious [...] And for others "queer" conjures up those awful memories of adolescent suffering [...] Well, yes, "gay" is great. It has its place. But when a lot of lesbians and gay men wake up in the morning we feel angry and disgusted, not gay. So we've chosen to call ourselves queer. Using "queer" is a way of reminding us how we are perceived by the rest of the world".

Note, though, that for some people—especially older people—'queer' can hold negative connotations as it was exclusively a discriminatory term in the past.

Questioning: This is used to describe people who identify as non-heterosexual and are still exploring or questioning their gender or sexual orientation but who do not wish to identify with other labels.

Marriage: This term is preferred for referencing legally binding matrimony. When talking about rights for same-sex marriage, the term 'marriage equality' is generally accepted.

Out: This term is preferred over 'admitted homosexual', 'admitted lesbian', and similar constructions, which can be viewed as negative terms. The opposite, 'not out' is preferred over 'in the closet', or 'closeted'.

While not widely accepted by advocacy groups, 'openly gay', 'openly lesbian', and similar constructs are commonly used in the news, and, especially to describe the first of something, such as 'first openly gay candidate for President'.

Transgender: This term encompasses many gender identities to describe those who don't identify with their sex assigned at birth—either partially or exclusively. The term is not indicative of gender expression, sexual orientation, hormonal makeup, physical anatomy, or how one is perceived in daily life.

Avoid expressing 'transgender' as a singular noun, such as "She is a transgender". Likewise, avoid referencing transgender people as 'biologically male/fame', 'genetically male/female', or 'born a man/woman'. Instead, the preferred terms are 'designated/assigned male/female at birth'.

Collecting Personal Information

When collecting personal information about people, including gender, it's common practice to provide additional options for the respondent to choose.

✎ Example

What is your gender?

[ ] Woman

[ ] Man

[ ] Self-described (please specify): _____

Quick Tips:

- Use 'different sex' instead of 'opposite sex' (as this recognizes 'gender' as a spectrum rather than as binary).
- Avoid guessing gender identity, marital status, or sexual orientation. When in doubt, reconsider the need to include this information.
- Avoid using words such as 'wife' or 'husband' that assumes heterosexual relationships as the norm.
- When using pronouns, it's best practice to use the pronoun preferred by the subject rather than their gender assigned at birth. If unsure, use collective pronouns such as 'they,' 'their', and 'them'.
- When addressing letters, written invitations, or emails, try to use the title that person uses, which may mean using the title they use in their correspondence. If you don't know what title they use, it's also acceptable to address someone by their first and last names.

List of preferred terms:

Sample Term	Preferred Equivalent	Sample Term	Preferred Equivalent
different sex	opposite sex	admitted gay/lesbian/etc	out
in the closet	not out	homophobia	prejudice
homosexual	gay	gay rights	civil rights for gay people
biologically male/female genetically male/female born a man/woman	designated/assigned male/female at birth	bi	bisexual

6

PEOPLE WITH DISABILITIES

According to the Society of Professional Journalists, 20% of the U.S. population has a physical and/or mental disability, making this subgroup of users one of the largest minorities in your audience to consider.

Among those with a disability around the world, there any many types and different attitudes regarding how they view their disability. This in turn can make language a sensitive issue. Terms such as 'wheelchair-bound/confined', for example, don't represent the experience of all wheelchair users. Many wheelchair users see their wheelchair as a source of mobility and increased independence.

Thus, in most cases, you want to avoid language that frames disability as a personal limitation. This also means a person should not be defined by their disability or described as a 'victim' or 'suffering', which is in contrast to how people with a disability are typically portrayed.

Next, person-first language is widely accepted when referring to people with a disability. This means writing 'people with a disability' rather than 'disabled people' or 'the handicapped'. In addition, some advocates (for people with a disability) cite the etymology of the term 'handicapped' as derived from someone "who had to beg with a cap in his or her hand because of the inability to maintain employment". 'Disabled' is therefore the preferred alternative to describe someone with a disability.

Quick Tips:
- Avoid language that implies people with disabilities are victims or are inspirations for living with a disability.

- Consider whether referring to a person's disability is relevant (in many cases, it might not).
- Avoid expressions that refer to mental illness such as 'crazy', 'that was mental', 'she went completely psycho', etc.
- Use 'person with a disability' or 'people with a disability' as the collective term rather than 'the disabled'.
- Avoid terms that reinforce a limitation such as 'the handicapped', 'midget', and 'cripple'. See an extended list below.

List of preferred terms:

Sample Term	Preferred Equivalent	Sample Term	Preferred Equivalent
the handicapped	people with disabilities	midget	person of short status
impaired | crippled	person with a disability	wheelchair-bound	person who uses a wheelchair
autistic child	a child with autism	retarded	person with intellectual development disability
crazy | insane | psycho	a person with mental illness	the blind	people with vision impairments
the deaf	people with hearing impairments		

7

AGEISM

Ageism, also called age discrimination, is described by the World Health Organization (WHO) as "stereotyping, prejudice, and discrimination against people based on their age".[5]

Ageism has wide implications and is known to have a negative effect on finding employment, applying for a new credit card or car insurance, gaining membership to a club or association, and can have a significant impact on one's overall confidence and quality of life.

Unfortunately, ageism is widespread but isn't as well-recognized as other social issues such as racism and sexism, which limits public rallying and awareness-raising. The WHO, though, places the number of older people above 60 years of age as 2 billion by 2050—almost doubling from 12% in 2015 to 22% in 2050—which underlines the relevance and importance of countering how elderly people are currently treated.

Ageism can be seen in how older people are represented in the media, which tends to reinforce older people as 'frail' and 'dependent'. This can lead older people to feel and perceive their lives as less valuable or as a burden on society. In combination with the marginalization experienced in communities, this has a negative impact on the health and well-being of older people and increases their risk of depression and social isolation. Research by Levy et al estimates that people's life expectancy increases 7.5 years when "one thinks positively about aging".[6]

---

[5] 'Ageing and Life-course', *World Health Organization*,
https://www.who.int/ageing/ageism/en/
[6] International Day of Older Persons 2016, *World Health Organization*
https://www.who.int/ageing/events/idop_rationale/en/

Ageism also creeps into language through age-based stereotypes such as 'grumpy old man' and other exaggerated traits. Thus, it's best to reframe from stereotyping and derogatory phrases that embrace or embellish those stereotypes, such as "you sound like an old woman" or "you complain like an old person".

Aside from avoiding negative stereotypes, it's important to stay away from expressions that refer to a person's age (except for referring to specific age groups including retirees and children) and to avoid negative terms (i.e. 'geriatric', 'fogey').

Quick Tips:

- Don't use women or an older relative as a substitute for 'novice' or 'beginner'. For example, don't say "something is so simple to use your mother (or grandpa) could do it".
- 'Older persons' or 'seniors' are usually preferred terms over saying 'the elderly'.
- For describing technology and computer operations, it's important to provide clear instructions and explanations of technical terms and consider the needs of the elderly when writing such content.
- Avoid negative terms such as 'over the hill', 'little old lady', 'grandfathering', 'fogey', or 'geriatric'.

List of preferred terms:

Sample Term	Preferred Equivalent
the elderly	over the hill	older person	senior
little old lady	a lady mature in age and small in stature
geriatric	a person in their 80s/90s

8

FOR OTHER GROUPS

Beyond the five groups mentioned by chapter in this book, inclusive language extends to other groups and identities. This includes groups defined by their socio-economic status, family status, criminal record, or religion.

Many of the key principles applied in earlier chapters apply to talking about other groups of people. This translates to avoiding loaded language, stereotypes, and assumptions, using specific descriptions, and choosing appropriate words to describe groups of people.

Describing someone who has spent time in prison as a 'convicted felon', for example, carries a loaded meaning, whereas a more inclusive way of saying this is 'a person who was formally incarcerated' or 'a person who formally served time in prison'.

The description of the person should also be specific and mention the grounds for their incarceration as there is a broad spectrum of crimes ranging from rape and homicide to tax evasion and providing refuge to a person after they have committed a crime.

Example

"As someone who served time in prison for tax evasion, [insert name] is now turning a new leaf by helping other business owners to avoid the same fate".

Writing for a Global Audience

As your platform, organization, or online audience expands on a global scale, it's important to communicate in a voice that isn't specific to one region. Naturally, this tip doesn't apply to content tailored to a specific area such as Europe or New York City.

When writing for a global audience, it is important to consider that your audience spans a diverse blend of nationalities, ages, ethnicities, family statuses, religions, political views, and socio-economic backgrounds.

Quick Tips:

- When translating and converting a topic written originally for an audience in one country, you may need to tailor the content to fit a global audience and perspective.
- When you use words in your content from other languages with non-Romanized alphabetical characters, such as Arabic, Japanese, and Farsi, it's important to add an accompanying Romanized version of the word to aid English-speaking users.
- When quoting prices for a global audience, it's useful to use US Dollars and not a local currency unless specific to currency exchange or another relevant scenario. Naturally, content that is specific to a region or country may use the local denomination for that region/country.
- Avoid idioms, colloquial expressions, and culture-specific references that might be confusing for non-native English speakers to understand, i.e. 'a piece of cake'.
- Avoid referring to season as they occur at different times in different parts of the world, while some regions do not have seasons. Instead, use months or calendar quarters to talk about time periods.

Writing for a Local Audience

Inclusive language also means anticipating a diverse audience at a local level and making a conscious effort to reflect that diversity in written communication and images.

Inclusive language can vary depending on whether you are a local government body in one part of the country or another organization addressing a national audience. Whether on a local or national level, it's important to use inclusive language, avoid stereotypes, labels and assumptions, and to use specific descriptions.

In Australia, for example, the inclusive collective term for Indigenous Australians is 'Aboriginal and Torres Strait Islander peoples'. In Canada, meanwhile, 'Aboriginal Peoples' is usually preferred as 'Native People' or 'First Nations People' do not fully encompass the diverse origins and identities of the various groups. In America, the Race Forward organization refers to the native people of America as 'American Indian' and 'Native American'.

9

YOUR TURN: A NAMING EXERCISE

Having reviewed and discussed different aspects of inclusive language, it's time to apply this knowledge with a practical exercise of naming a new product.

About the Product

Imagine you work for a mobile app company in an English-speaking country with an international user base. Your task as a Content Strategist or Product Designer is to name the new version for an existing app.

This new version of the app has been specially designed to enhance the user experience of the original app by integrating larger font, buttons, and icons as well as a simplified layout with reduced content on the homepage, and removal of distracting pop-up banners.

The new version of the app does not change the core functions of the app; it is simply an optional or alternative version of the original app. Users can opt to switch to the new version within the Settings menu of the app, without needing to download a new app to their device.

The development and design of this new version have come in response to feedback from users about accessibility problems and comments such as the following:

"Why does the font have to be so small? It's extremely difficult for my mother-in-law to navigate."

"The homepage—with so many icons—can be quite disorientating for older users as there is no clear direction of where to tap first."

> *"Extremely hard to navigate. Too many distractions!!"*

In this chapter, your task is to name the new version of the app with the goal of enabling more users to enjoy the app's core features while being respectful and inclusive.

Task 1

Take a few minutes to brainstorm ideas for naming the new version of the app. If possible, take note of why you selected these names and whether they comply with the principles and best practices discussed in this book.

Task 2

While the names you came up with provide a suitable solution, your boss insists on adopting one of their own suggestions. Based on your boss's suggestions, you now need to vote for the best option (listed below) in line with the original goal of enabling more users to enjoy the app while being respectful and inclusive.

Your boss's suggestions:

a. Seniors Mode

b. Geriatric Mode

c. Larger Text Mode

d. Easy Mode

Based on your existing knowledge of inclusive language and your understanding of the product, which of the above options will you advise or nudge your boss towards choosing?

Solutions

As you may have encountered, there isn't a perfect solution for this second task. There are drawbacks associated with each option and this dilemma is indicative of working in the real world and outside of theoretical boundaries.

Regardless, let's proceed by discussing some of the considerations behind each naming option.

a) Seniors Mode

While "seniors" is generally an accepted term for referring to older users, this name comes with two major drawbacks. The first drawback is that not all senior users have low vision and/or a low level of tech literacy. The name "Seniors Mode" carries a general assumption that older users have poor eyesight and cannot navigate technology with the same ease and savviness as younger users. The second problem with this name is that it doesn't connect and relate with younger users with impaired vision and who could benefit from using the new version of the app.

b) Geriatric Mode

Given that "geriatric" is typically tied to negative stereotypes of older people and is not inclusive of younger users, this is not a suitable name for the new version of the app.

c) Larger Text Mode

Larger Text Mode is inclusive of younger and older users who could benefit from the new app and does not cast a negative stereotype on any particular user group. One drawback, however, is that larger text is just one of several new features, along with larger icons, a simplified layout, and the removal of distracting pop-up banners. Hence, while the name Larger Text Mode is inclusive of different types of users, there could be pushback from the company's design and product teams who feel the name doesn't do justice to their full creation.

d) Easy Mode

Similar to Larger Text Mode, Easy Mode is inclusive of different types of users and does not cast a stereotype based on age or disability. At the same time, this name is likely to meet pushback from colleagues that worry over the name reflecting negatively on the original version of the app. In other words, if the new version of the app is named "Easy", users may construe the original version of the app as "not easy" or "hard". This is one of the challenges of using an adjective with an obvious antonym. Other adjective-based names such as "Clean Mode" and "Simple Mode" might also imply that the original version of the app is "not clean" or "not simple".

Summary

In short, naming a new product or a service that satisfies both marketing needs and inclusivity is challenging and sometimes there isn't a distinct or clear solution. For situations in which other parties are pushing towards a name that emphasizes marketing interests at the expense of inclusivity, you should be prepared to provide feedback using inclusive language guidelines or case studies from other organizations.

One potential case study that we could point to is "Be My Eyes". This is a free app that connects blind and low-vision people with sighted volunteers for visual assistance through a live video call.

The name of this app is a great example of using words that stay clear of limiting stereotypes while also intuitively describing the product at hand.

While we should not directly copy this name for our own product, we can use "Be My Eyes" as an example of finding a creative solution and thinking outside the box. We might also want to add the name to our swipe file. Who knows, we might adapt the name for an audio-assistance product called "Be My Ears" in the future, for instance.

10

NEXT STEPS

While it might seem complex, incorporating inclusive language into your organization's content or your own communication takes less effort than you might think. Habits around word choice can be quickly adapted as you become conscious of inclusive and exclusive terms. Nor should inclusive language discourage or prevent you from developing your own original and unique writing and communication style. For instance, there are many ways to implement gender-inclusive language that you can adopt to fit your own communication style.

Avoiding stereotypes in your writing and verbal communication also opens your mindset and perspective about other people. It makes you dig deeper into understanding another person's background rather than classifying that person based on one monolithic group, such as gay, black, or old. You learn to see their uniqueness and appreciate who they are as an individual person.

Creating an Inclusive Language Guide

One of the best ways to implement inclusive language at work or within your organization is to create an inclusive language guide and to borrow liberally from the contents covered in this book. Alternatively, you may like to find your own resources and create your own guidelines based on your audience.

As much as possible, try to keep the document live and encourage others to add their input and feedback which will also help to give them ownership and buy-in over implementing and maintaining those guidelines.

This guide can take the form of a shareable PowerPoint presentation, PDF, or another format. You may even like to share the basic principles of your guide publicly on your website as a reference for others. (First, though, you may need to conduct an audit of your existing content and update any instances that contradict your values and new guidelines on inclusion and diversity.)

11

CHECKLIST

1) Does the content make assumptions or reinforce stereotypes about a user's sexual orientation, gender, race, marital status, religion, or age?

2) Can I improve the gender balance by using male and female examples or gender-neutral language?

3) Is the content written for a global audience? If no, is there a reason for this? (i.e. content is only for users living in Europe).

4) Are there any words that could be interpreted as offensive to my audience? I.E. blacklist, crazy prices, manpower, old man, invasion, etc.

5) Are the accompanying images or banners consistent with our mission to promote diversity and avoid stereotypes?

6) Is the text clearly legible and easy to read, including for people who are colorblind?

12

THANK YOU

Thank you. We hope you found value in this brief guide to inclusive language.

To the best of our knowledge, this is the first book dedicated to the topic of inclusive language published on Amazon.com. While this title is much shorter than what you would expect from a standard size book, we feel it's important that this topic is covered on Amazon, and we hope to see this genre grow in the future.

The way we write and speak has a large impact on the way we think, and promoting inclusive language is a powerful channel to promote empathy and empowered participation. You can achieve this by putting yourself in the shoes of a diverse audience and trying to understand who you are seeking to address. As an example, if your race/ethnicity, age, marital status, sexual orientation, disabled status wasn't relevant to the content or the data being discussed, would you want it to be mentioned? How would that make you feel?

Sometimes, by highlighting or sensationalizing the achievements of a person with a disability or a given sexual orientation, we are saying this case is special or uncommon and contradictory to what we might expect from that group of people. We therefore need to be careful about the intended effects of dwelling on one aspect of someone's background.

On the other hand, inclusion doesn't mean we should ignore a factual situation. Children with developmental disabilities, for example, require special assistance, which necessitates the need to clearly communicate this information in school application forms or other relevant forms of communication. The key here is to be respectful and use words that are not derogatory or offensive such as 'mentally retarded' or 'under-developed'.

As with crafting good marketing copy or creating sentences that flow from one clause to another, it's vital to think about what different words mean, what type of image they create in the mind of the reader, and be willing to adapt to new practices. As mentioned, this book is not meant to be a comprehensive or prescriptive handbook to inclusive language. Discrepancies or contradictions are likely to arise over time and a big part of inclusive language is accepting the constant need for improvement.

Virtually no one can get language right 100 percent of the time for 100 percent of people. The important thing is to continue learning, update your inclusive language guide when necessary, and if you make a mistake, quickly apologize and improve your writing and communication skills for next time.

Contact us at lingovalley@gmail.com

12

BIBLIOGRAPHY

Ageing and life-course, World Health Organization, accessed July 14, 2020,
https://www.who.int/ageing/ageism/en/

Beth Haller, 'Covering Disability Issues', Society of Professional Journalists, accessed July 12, 2020, https://www.spj.org/dtb5.asp

Deborah Cameron, 'Feminism and Linguistic Theory', *Palgrave Macmillan*, 2nd Edition, 1992.

'Ageing and Life-course', *World Health Organization*, https://www.who.int/ageing/ageism/en/

'International Day of Older Persons 2016', *World Health Organization*

https://www.who.int/ageing/events/idop_rationale/en/

George Floyd: Twitter drops 'master', 'slave' and 'blacklist', The BBC, accessed July 22, 2020,
https://www.bbc.com/news/business-53273923

'Guide to Inclusive Language', RMIT Diversity and Inclusion, accessed July 2, 2020.

Inclusive language: words to use and avoid when writing about disability, UK Gov, accessed July 2, 2020,
https://www.gov.uk/government/publications/inclusive-communication/inclusive-language-words-to-use-and-avoid-when-writing-about-disability

Jessica Murphy, 'Toronto professor Jordan Peterson takes on gender-neutral pronouns', BBC News, Nov. 14, 2016.

Judith D. Fischer, "Framing Gender: Federal Appellate Judges' Choices About Gender-Neutral Language," University of San Francisco Law Review, Winter 2009, Vol. 42, No. 3.

Queen's University, Inclusive Language Guidelines, accessed July 2, 2020, https://www.queensu.ca/styleguide/inclusivelanguage

Race Reporting Guide 2015, Race Forward, accessed July 12, 2020, https://www.raceforward.org/sites/default/files/Race%20Reporting%20Guide%20by%20Race%20Forward_V1.1.pdf

The Victorian Government, 'Introduction: LGBTIQ inclusive language in the VPS', accessed July 12, 2020, https://www.vic.gov.au/inclusive-language-guide

Printed in Great Britain
by Amazon

75272616R00031